Computer Language Handbooks

Lisp

Sheila Hughes

GW00384452

Pitman

Computer Handbooks

The complete list of titles in this series and the Pitman Pocket Guide series appears after the Index at the end of this Handbook. The Publishers welcome suggestions for further additions and improvements to the series. Please write to Peter Brown at the address given below.

PITMAN PUBLISHING LIMITED
128 Long Acre, London WC2E 9AN

A Longman Group Company

© Sheila Hughes 1986

First edition 1986

British Library Cataloguing in Publication Data

Hughes, Sheila
   LISP. — (Computer language handbooks)
   1. LISP (Computer program language)
   I. Title   II. Series
   005.13'3   QA76.73.L23

   ISBN 0–273–02392–6

Printed in Great Britain at the Bath Press, Avon

Contents

How to Use this Handbook

This Handbook describes the dialect of Lisp known as Common Lisp. The complete definition of this dialect is set out in *Common Lisp – The Language* by Guy L Steele Jr, published by Digital Press 1984.

We cannot hope to cover all of Common Lisp's facilities in this Handbook; but we believe that all the major categories of facilities central to programming in Lisp are described.

Notation

When a Lisp function or special term is referred to by name in the text, it is written in capitals. If, in describing a function's behaviour, it is not stated explicitly whether or not the function's arguments are evaluated before the process body is entered, then the default can be assumed to be that the arguments *are* evaluated. The symbol **Lisp**> is the Lisp interpreter prompt; expressions on the same line as this prompt represent the user input.

Comments in Lisp code

Any characters which follow a semi-colon on any given line will be ignored by the Lisp interpreter. Thus comments may be entered into files of Lisp code. The semi-colon format is also used to annotate Lisp code in this Handbook

Arithmetic in Lisp

Numerical calculations in Lisp

Common Lisp is capable of handling several
numerical types.
These include:
- floating point numbers
- integers
- rational numbers (e.g. 22/7)

Arithmetic operations

Those available include:

```
(+ X Y Z ...)   ; arbitrary number of arguments
(− X Y Z ...)   ; all subsequent arguments subtracted
                ; from X
(* X Y Z ...)   ; multiplication
(/ X Y Z ...)   ; division of X by all subsequent
                ; arguments
(/ X)           ; gives reciprocal of X
```

If the arguments to the division operator are integers
and the result is non-integer, a rational number is
produced.
e.g. (/ 3 4 5) yields 3/20

```
(GCD X Y Z ...)   ; greatest common divisor of
                  ; arguments
(LCM X Y Z ...)   ; least common multiple of
                  ; arguments
```

Exponential and logarithmic functions

Those available include:
```
(EXP X)     ; e to the power of X
(EXPT X Y)  ; X to the power of Y
(LOG X)     ; natural logarithm of X
(LOG X Y)   ; log X to base Y
(SQRT X)    ; square root of X, X > 0
```

Trigonometric functions

Those available include:

```
(SIN X), (COS X), (TAN X)    ; X in radians
(ASIN X), (ACOS X), (ATAN X)
(SINH X), (COSH X), (TANH X)
(ASINH X), (ACOSH X), (ATANH X)
```

Logic and Predicates

In Lisp, a predicate is a function which tests for some condition involving its arguments. A predicate returns NIL if the condition is not met ('false') and some non-nil value if the condition is met.

While the Boolean 'false' has a unique representation in Lisp (i.e. NIL), any other Lisp value has the force of the logical 'true'. Hence, if a predicate succeeds, it should return the most useful or informative non-nil value possible. In the absence of a more interesting result, the 'standard' true value of Lisp, T, is returned.

Thus, a predicate returns a Boolean true/false value, although a Boolean 'true' in Lisp can in fact carry other information. Since predicates return Boolean values, logical conditions can be formed by the use of AND, OR and NOT.

(NOT NIL) always evaluates to T.
(NOT T) evaluates to NIL; but in fact any expression which is non-NIL, will, in conjunction with NOT, yield NIL.

Examples
Lisp> (NOT 4)
NIL

LISP> (NOT 0)
NIL

Lisp> (NOT 'APPLE)
NIL

Some commonly used Lisp predicates for numeric arguments are listed below.

```
(PLUSP X)    ; arg > 0?
(MINUSP X)   ; arg < 0?
(ZEROP X)    ; arg = 0?
(NUMBERP X)
(ODDP X)
(EVENP X)
(> X Y Z ...)  ; arguments in strictly descending
             ; order of magnitude
(< X Y Z ...)  ; ascending order of magnitude
(= X Y Z ...)  ; arguments are all the same
(/= X Y Z ...) ; arguments are all different
```

Lisp Variables and Value Assignments

Any non-numeric Lisp symbol can have a value assigned to it, and hence act as a 'variable'.

When the interpreter is presented with a Lisp symbol, it will attempt to evaluate it, i.e. return the symbol's value, unless we explicitly prevent it from doing so by 'quoting' the symbol.

If we wish to assign a value to a variable, the variable must first be 'declared' to the system. This is done using the special form **DEFVAR.**

```
Lisp> (DEFVAR A)    ; this argument is not
A                   ; evaluated!
```

We can, optionally, assign an initial value to the variable when we declare it:

```
Lisp> (DEFVAR B 'BROCCOLI)
B            ; Second argument evaluated.
Lisp> B
BROCCOLI
```

If, by chance, a variable has already been declared and has a value, and we re-declare it, the initial value given is *not* evaluated and assigned to the variable; after all, it cannot be an *initial* value if a value already exists!

```
Lisp> (DEFVAR B 'BREAD)
B
Lisp> B
BROCCOLI
```

Once declared, the value of a variable can be changed using the **SETQ** function. SETQ evaluates only its second argument.

For example:

```
Lisp> (SETQ B 'BANANA)
BANANA

Lisp> B
BANANA
```

Numeric symbols cannot be used as variables, because they are 'constants', i.e. the value assigned to this type of symbol cannot be altered. The value of a constant is the same as the symbol name, so we do not need to quote constants.

```
Lisp> (DEFVAR X 5)
X
Lisp> X
5
```

The symbol 5 which is presented as the second argument *is* being evaluated, so it does not alter our view of the DEFVAR function, and its value is **5.**

The function SETQ will handle any number of pairs of arguments. Hence we can write, after declaring the variables:

```
Lisp> (SETQ C 'CARROT D 'DAHLIA E 'EGG)
EGG
```

6

Assignment occurs pairwise from left to right, so CARROT becomes assigned to the symbol C before any further arguments are evaluated. This means we can rely on the values of symbols assigned earlier within the same SETQ.
For example:

```
Lisp> (SETQ F 'FLOUR G F)
FLOUR
```

First, the arguments F and 'FLOUR are considered. 'FLOUR evaluates to FLOUR, and FLOUR is then assigned to the symbol F. Next, the arguments G and F and considered. F evaluates to FLOUR (since it has just been successfully assigned), and so FLOUR is then assigned to the symbol G.

There is a function similar to SETQ which operates in a rather different manner. It is **PSETQ**. When PSETQ has multiple pairs of arguments, argument evaluation and assignment proceed in parallel, not in a left-to-right fashion. Consider the following:

```
Lisp> (SETQ K 'KALE L 'LEMON)
LEMON
Lisp> K
KALE
Lisp> L
LEMON
Lisp> (PSETQ K L L K)
NIL
Lisp> K
LEMON
Lisp> L
KALE
```

In the call to PSETQ, the second and fourth arguments were both evaluated *before* any assignment took place; hence the value assigned to L by using the second pair of arguments is the old value of K, not the new one created by the first pair of arguments. Note the difference from:

```
Lisp> (SETQ K L L K)
LEMON
Lisp> K
LEMON
Lisp> L
LEMON        ; the new value of K
```

The SETQ function is the 'simple variable assignment statement' of Lisp.

In the rest of the handbook, we will assume that any variables being assigned to by SETQ have already been declared using DEFVAR.

Lists and Functions

Lists in Lisp are formed by surrounding the constituent elements with parentheses, for example:

(2   4   6   8)   is a list of four elements
(5 3 (7 6 4) 8)   is a list of four elements, the third of
                  which is a list of three elements.

When a list is evaluated, it is treated in a special way. The first element is then said to be in the functional place, and the subsequent elements are regarded as arguments to that function, for example:

(SETQ X (QUOTE GOLD))

This is a list of three elements; when it is evaluated, the first element, SETQ is recognised as a function. Its *functional binding* is examined: this stands in contrast to the *value binding* of a symbol. (There is no reason why SETQ could not also have a value, from a previous command, e.g. (SETQ SETQ 'CARROT).) The second element, X, is not evaluated – the directives contained in SETQ's functional binding control this. The third element is a list, (QUOTE GOLD), and this is evaluated. Once again, we have a list under evaluation, so QUOTE is treated as a function. The QUOTE function takes one argument, and returns that argument without evaluation. Thus (QUOTE GOLD) has exactly the same effect as 'GOLD. Having evaluated any arguments appropriate, the functional binding of SETQ causes the value of the symbol X to be set to the symbol GOLD. An evaluated function always returns a value – a 'result' or 'output', if you like – and in the case of SETQ, this is the value of the second argument.

If the first element in a list under evaluation does not have a function binding, an error will be generated. For example:

```
Lisp> (WEIRD 'A)
Fatal Error
Symbol has no function definition: WEIRD
```

Well-formed Lisp Expressions

Any well-formed Lisp object is called an **s-expression,** which is an abbreviation for 'symbolic expression'.

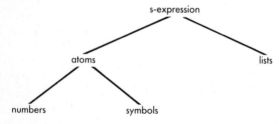

Numbers

Three distinguishable types of number can be represented in Common Lisp.

Integers
These may be signed or unsigned, and are normally

10

written in base 10. However, any radix from 2 to 36 (inclusive) may be used as follows:

    #2R1101; decimal 13, base 2.
    #25R-7H; decimal −192, base 25.

Since binary, octal and hexadecimal bases may be especially useful, special representations are available for each.
Hence,

    #B1101 = #2R1101 = decimal 13
    #O325 = #8R325 = decimal 213
    #XD5 = #16RD5 = decimal 213

Any required sign is written after the radix information, e.g.

    #B-1101 = decimal −13

Ratios
Common Lisp can represent rational numbers: the mathematical ratio of two integers. These may be signed or unsigned, for example:

    22/7   −1/3

The denominator may *not* be zero. Common Lisp will accept unreduced ratios, e.g. 4/6, but will refer to them in canonical (reduced) form. So the evaluation of

    (/4 6)

will yield 2/3.

If a computation on rational numbers produces a result which can be reduced to a rational with denominator 1, the result is automatically converted into an integer. This is called *rational canonicalisation*, for example:

```
Lisp> (* 5/2 −4/5)
−2
```

The integers used to describe a rational number may be represented in bases other than 10; the rules for this are described in the section above. The radix, however, refers to both the numerator and denominator, for example:

```
#3R121/21 = decimal 16/7
#B101/10 = decimal 5/2
```

Floating-point numbers
Floating-point numbers may be signed or unsigned, and can be written in either decimal fraction or in an exponential form.

Examples:

```
3.142
6.02E+23    ; Avogadro's number
60.2E+22    ; ditto
602E+21     ; ditto
−272.8
```

Symbolic atoms

The construction rules for the names of this type of s-expression are specific to the dialect of Lisp.

Common Lisp is *not* case-sensitive; all alphabetic characters are translated internally into the uppercase equivalent. Hence the following are all treated identically:

```
(SETQ A 5)
(setq a 5)
(Setq a 5)
```

Symbol names can be constructed using alphabetic characters, numerals, and any of the following symbols:

```
 + − * / @ $ % ^ & _ \ < > ~.
```

The only syntactic restriction on these special characters is that a symbol name may not consist entirely of periods.

Spaces, parentheses and carriage returns are all delimiters within Lisp, and thus it is illegal to include them in a symbol value.
The characters:

```
 ? ! [ ] { }
```

are reserved for special purposes; it is strongly recommended that they are *not* included in symbolic names; although, strictly speaking, it is not syntactically illegal.

Symbolic atoms may have a value assigned to them, or they may be unbound.

They may also have a function binding.

A symbolic atom may also have a property list assigned to it. This is discussed in the section entitled Property Lists on p. 74.

Lists

A list is contained within parentheses, and has zero or more elements, each of which is a Lisp s-expression. Each element is separated from the next by at least one space.

We have already seen that when a list is the argument presented to EVAL, the first element of that list is in the functional position. If the s-expression in the functional position is a symbolic atom, the function binding is examined. If there is a sublist in the functional position, EVAL will produce an error, since a list cannot have an associated function binding.

List Manipulation

Lists are stored in list cells. Each list cell has two parts, and it is possible to store two values per list cell, thus:

This is legitimate, and it is called a **CONS** or **DOTTED PAIR.** It is written (A . B).

N.B. (A.B) is not a CONS, it is a list of one element, A.B.

We cannot, however, add another element to a CONS. In the usual list structure employed in Lisp, only one value is stored per list cell and the second part of the cell houses a pointer to the next element in the list.

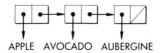

APPLE   AVOCADO   AUBERGINE

To enable us to access the various portions of a list, we employ two functions with unfortunately non-mnemonic names.

CAR is a function which takes one argument, which must be a list. It returns the first element of that list.

```
Lisp> (SETQ A '(APPLE AVOCADO AUBERGINE))
       (APPLE AVOCADO AUBERGINE)

Lisp> (CAR A)
APPLE

Lisp> (CAR A) ; NB The function CAR has not
APPLE          ; altered the value of the argument.

Lisp> (CAR '((MELON MANGO) (ORANGE
       OKRA) (FENNEL FIG)) )
(MELON MANGO)
```

By definition, the CAR of an empty list is an empty list.

CDR also takes one argument, which must be a list. It returns a list of all the elements except the CAR.

```
Lisp> (CDR A)
(AVOCADO AUBERGINE)

Lisp> (CDR '((MELON MANGO) ( ORANGE
      OKRA) (FENNEL FIG)) )
((ORANGE OKRA) (FENNEL FIG))
```

By definition, the CDR of an empty list is an empty list.

If we wish to access, say, FENNEL in our second example, we could write

```
Lisp> (CAR (CDR (CDR '((MELON MANGO)
      (ORANGE OKRA) (FENNEL FIG)) )))
FENNEL
```

… but this can be painful if the list structure is deeply nested. Common Lisp therefore will accept modifications to the function names CAR and CDR, thus:

```
Lisp> (CADDR '((MELON MANGO) (ORANGE
      OKRA) (FENNEL FIG)) )))
FENNEL
```

A maximum total of four A's and D's can be employed, and are examined from right to left as the example shows. Hence, valid function names include CADR, CDADR, CDAR, CDDDDR, etc, but not CAAADDR – it has more than four A's and D's.

N.B. CAR and CDR – and their unpronounceable offspring – have no effect on the value bindings of their arguments. That is, the value of A will remain as (APPLE AVOCADO AUBERGINE) after any number of CAR or CDR operations.

We can update the value of a variable using SETQ thus:

```
Lisp> (SETQ A 'APPLE)
APPLE
```

But suppose we wish to update an object which is not simply the value of a variable? If we can describe a *location* in which a unique s-expression may reside, we are permitted to update the contents of that location using **SETF.** For example, the CAR and CDR of a list:

```
Lisp> (SETQ X '(1 2 (3 4) 5 6))
(1 2 (3 4) 5 6)
Lisp> (SETF (CAR X) '(A B))
((A B) 2 (3 4) 5 6)
Lisp> X
((A B) 2 (3 4) 5 6)
Lisp> (SETF (CADDR X) 'P)
((A B) 2 P 5 6)
```

SETF may be used with a symbol name, since that too describes a location.

```
Lisp> (SETF Y '(7 6 5))
(7 6 5)
Lisp> Y
(7 6 5)
```

So SETF subsumes the function of SETQ. Note that the first argument to SETF is not evaluated: it is used to describe a location.

We use SETF as an all-purpose update function. It can be used for any Lisp structure. It does, however, require that access functions can be defined for the structure in question just as CAR and CDR are access functions for lists.

List Construction

CONS is a Lisp function which takes two arguments. It makes the first argument the CAR of the second argument. Hence, the second argument should be a list. If it is not, CONS does not however return an error, but constructs a dotted pair.

```
Lisp> (CONS 'APRICOT A)
(APRICOT APPLE AVOCADO AUBERGINE)

Lisp> A
(APPLE AVOCADO AUBERGINE)

Lisp> (CONS 'APRICOT 'APPLE)
(APRICOT . APPLE)
```

Like CAR and CDR, CONS has no side effects on the values of its arguments. The empty list can be used to good effect with CONS.

```
Lisp> (CONS 'APRICOT '() )
(APRICOT)
Lisp> (CONS A NIL)    ; NIL is equivalent to the
                      ; empty list ()

((APPLE AVOCADO AUBERGINE))  ; Note extra
                             ; parentheses
```

LIST is a function which can take any number of arguments. The value of each argument becomes a top-level element in a new list returned by LIST.

```
Lisp> (LIST 'CHERRY 'COCONUT)
(CHERRY COCONUT)

Lisp> (LIST 'APRICOT A 'ARTICHOKE 'ALFALFA)
(APRICOT (APPLE AVOCADO AUBERGINE)
ARTICHOKE ALFALFA)
```

LIST has no effect on the value bindings of its arguments.

APPEND takes an arbitrary number of arguments, each of which must be lists in their own right. Each top-level element from each argument becomes a top-level element in a single list which is returned by APPEND.

Lisp> (SETQ B '(BANANA BEAN))
(BANANA BEAN)

Lisp> (SETQ C '(CHERRY COCONUT))
(CHERRY COCONUT)

Lisp> (APPEND C B)
(CHERRY COCONUT BANANA BEAN)

Lisp> (APPEND () B)
(BANANA BEAN)

Lisp> (APPEND B NIL)
(BANANA BEAN)

Like CONS and LIST, APPEND has no effect on the value bindings of its arguments.

Equality and Identity

In Common Lisp, some s-expressions are very
definitely more 'equal' than others. There are in fact,
four distinct tests for 'equality', and it is important to
understand the differences between them in order to
select the appropriate test when programming.

The four predicates (for such they are) in order of
stringency are:

EQ (the most specific), **EQL, EQUAL** and **EQUALP**
(the most general)

If two objects satisfy one of these predicates, then
they will definitely satisfy all of the more general
forms.

EQ

Two objects are EQ if and only if they occupy the
same physical memory location. Non-numeric
symbols which have the same name are EQ, since
only one copy is held.

```
Lisp> (EQ 'A 'A)
T
Lisp> (SETQ X 'A)
A
Lisp> (EQ X X)
T
```

For numeric arguments of the same type, objects which look the same may or may not be physically identical; this depends entirely on the specific implementation of Common Lisp.

Hence, it is not possible in general to predict the result of the following comparisons:

```
(EQ 3 3)
(EQ 5.1 5.1)
```

We can, however, state categorically that the following comparisons will return NIL:

```
(EQ 3 3.0)
```

since the numeric arguments are of different *types*.

To determine whether two lists are EQ, it is necessary to understand something of how lists are constructed and held in memory.

Figures 1a, 1b and 1c illustrate the working of the CONS function, and show how two lists having the same constituent elements may not be EQ.

Unused memory cells are held on the *Free Storage List* (FSL). In Figure 1a we see that the value of A has been set to (APPLE AVOCADO AUBERGINE). In Figure 1b we see the effect of the following evaluation:

```
Lisp> (SETQ AA (CONS 'APRICOT A))
(APRICOT APPLE AVOCADO AUBERGINE)
```

Figure 1

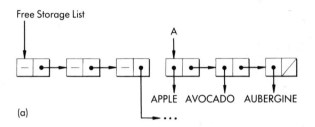

(a)

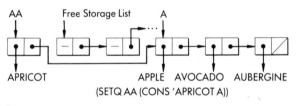

(SETQ AA (CONS 'APRICOT A))

(b)

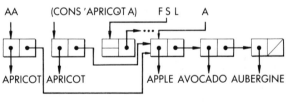

(c)

The first cell on the FSL has been used: it points to APRICOT, and its CDR points to the first element of A. The value binding of AA is attached to this new cell. So, we will now get the following identity confirmed:

```
Lisp> (EQ A (CDR AA))
T
```

... since A and the CDR of AA physically occupy the same cells.

If we now try the following:

```
Lisp> (EQ AA (CONS 'APRICOT A))   ; See Figure
NIL                                ; 1c
```

... the result is NIL because CONS does exactly as it did in Figure 1b; it takes another cell from the FSL and attaches it by its CDR to the first element of A. So, AA and the new (CONS 'APRICOT A) do not occupy the same memory cells, hence they cannot be EQ.

Figure 2 shows how, when using LIST to construct new lists, we obtain the following apparently odd result:

```
Lisp> (EQ (LIST B C) (LIST B C))
NIL
```

Figure 2

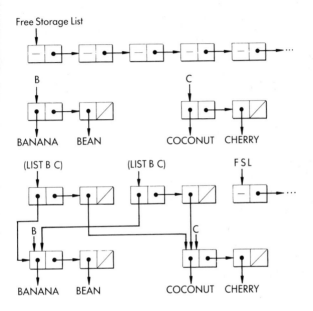

Each call to LIST creates a new list formed from cells from the FSL. Although the pointers from the new lists point to the same object, the pointers themselves are kept in physically separate memory cells.

25

For the sake of completeness, Figure 3 shows how
APPEND works. Copies are made of all arguments
save the last, in order that the end-of-list marker may
be changed to a pointer for each argument. If this
were done on the original lists, it would alter the
value bindings of every argument except the last
one.

Figure 3

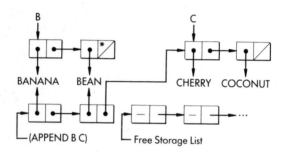

N.B.
Lisp> (EQ C (CDDR (APPEND B C)))
T   ; BECAUSE C has not been copied by APPEND

If the original lists were tampered with, the end of list
in B (marked with an asterisk) would be altered to a
pointer to the first cell of C. The subsequent value
binding of B would then become (BANANA BEAN
CHERRY COCONUT); which is not a desirable side
effect from APPEND.

EQL

This predicate is designed to overcome the implementation-specific difficulties encountered with EQ. It therefore acts in an exactly similar manner, *except* when dealing with comparisons of numbers. If two numbers of the same type are examined using EQL, then their *values* are compared, not their memory locations. So, we confidently predict that

```
(EQL 3 3)
(EQL 5.1 5.1)
```

will all be T.

However, the following example still fails the test, returning NIL.

```
(EQL 3 3.0)
```

EQL tests whether two objects are *conceptually* identical; EQ tests for *implementational* identity.

EQUAL

Two objects are, in general, EQUAL if they look the same when printed by the system. So, for numbers, EQUAL is as stringent as EQL, but for lists we now have a predicate which allows us the result:

```
Lisp> (EQUAL (LIST B C) (LIST B C))
T      ; see Figure 2
```

EQUALP

This is the most lax of the four equality predicates. It will ignore data types for numeric arguments and just compare their values; it even ignores case differences in alphabetic strings (*see* String Operations on p. 96).

```
Lisp> (EQUALP 3 3.0)
T
Lisp> (EQUALP "TOP" "top")
T
```

When the arguments are numeric, an 'equals' sign is commonly used; this has the same effect as EQUALP.

```
Lisp> (= 3 3.0)
T
```

N.B. It is an error to use the 'equals' sign with non-numeric arguments.

More List Accessing Functions

Further list accessing functions are introduced in this section. All of them can be written quite simply in terms of the more fundamental list processing functions which we have already met. However, in Common Lisp they are present in a machine-coded form for efficiency.

Unless otherwise specified, these functions take exactly *one* argument, which must evaluate to a list. None of them have any lasting side-effects.

LAST returns a list – not, please note, the element – containing the last top-level element of the input list. It can be thought of as the last CDR before the empty list is reached.

```
Lisp> (DEFVAR X '(APPLE (BANANA BEAN)
        CARROT) )
X
Lisp> (LAST X)
(CARROT)
```

NTH requires two arguments: a non-negative integer and a list. If the integer is i, then NTH returns the ith element of the list, where the CAR of the list counts as the zeroth element.

```
Lisp> (NTH 0 X)
APPLE
Lisp> (NTH 2 X)
CARROT
Lisp> (NTH 3 X)
NIL
Lisp> (NTH 27 X)
NIL
```

If the integer is greater than or equal to the list length, then NTH returns NIL.

There are ten named functions:

FIRST, SECOND THIRD, ... NINTH, TENTH.

These each return the appropriate list element, this time beginning the enumeration at one.

```
LISP> (FIRST X)
APPLE
i.e. (FIRST X) = (CAR X) = (NTH 0 X)
     (SECOND X) = (CADR X) = (NTH 1 X)
```

NTHCDR, like NTH, takes two arguments, a non-negative integer **i** and a list. NTHCDR performs the CDR operation **i** times on the list.

```
Lisp> (NTHCDR 0 X)
(APPLE (BANANA BEAN) CARROT)
Lisp> (NTHCDR 2 X)
(CARROT)
Lisp> (NTHCDR 3 X)
NIL
Lisp> (NTHCDR 23 X)
NIL
```

So we see that NTH and NTHCDR are related thus:

```
(CAR (NTHCDR N X)) = (NTH N X)
```

More List Operations

In this section are introduced some Common Lisp functions which aid in list manipulation. None of these functions permanently alters the value of its argument(s).

ENDP is a predicate to test for end-of-list. It is true for the argument NIL, false for any CONS, and produces an error for any other argument.
Note: There are three separately-named functions in Common Lisp which all perform more or less the same task. They are:

NULL, NOT and ENDP.

NULL and NOT do in fact act in precisely the same manner:

```
Lisp> (NULL NIL)      Lisp> (NOT NIL)
T                     T
Lisp> (NULL '() )     Lisp> (NOT '() )
T                     T
```

Both NULL and NOT yield NIL for any other argument. The choice of function depends on the intent of the programmer; when checking for the empty list, one should use NULL. When the intent is to use a logical operator, NOT should be employed. This gives a better programming style, making the final code more readable.
Since it is an error to give an atomic argument to ENDP, this function is recommended for use as a

termination condition for progressive reduction of a list. This should result in clearer, more robust code.

```
Lisp> (SETQ X '(ONE TWO))    ; X was declared
(ONE TWO)                     ; on p. 29
Lisp> (ENDP (CDR X))          ; (CDR X) = (TWO)
NIL
LISP> (ENDP (CDDR X))
T
```

LIST-LENGTH returns an integer which gives the number of top-level element in a list.

```
Lisp> (LIST-LENGTH X)
2
Lisp> (LIST-LENGTH '((1 2) (3 4)) )
2
Lisp> (LIST-LENGTH NIL)
0
```

REVERSE returns a list whose elements are those of the list given as the argument, except in reverse order.

```
Lisp> (REVERSE '(1 2 (3 4) 5) )
(5 (3 4) 2 1)
Lisp> (REVERSE NIL)
NIL
```

BUTLAST returns a list with its last element omitted.

```
Lisp> (BUTLAST '(1 2 (3 4) 5) )
(1 2 (3 4) )
Lisp> (BUTLAST '(APPLE) )
NIL                        ; the empty list
Lisp> (BUTLAST NIL)
NIL
```

Optionally, one can give a second argument to
BUTLAST. This should be a positive integer **j.** The
function then returns a list with the last **j** elements
omitted.

```
Lisp> (BUTLAST '(1 2 (3 4) 5)  3)
(1)
Lisp> (BUTLAST '(1 2 (3 4) 5)  8)
NIL
```

SUBST requires three arguments: a new pattern to be substituted in; the old pattern; and the (possibly nested) list. The new pattern is substituted for the old throughout the list, but there are no lasting side effects.

```
Lisp>  (DEFVAR MTREE
         '((MAMMAL DOG CAT HORSE)
           (DOG SPANIEL COLLIE TERRIER)
           (CAT BURMESE)) )
(...)

Lisp> (SUBST 'CANIS 'DOG MTREE)
((MAMMAL CANIS CAT HORSE)
 (CANIS SPANIEL COLLIE TERRIER)
 (CAT BURMESE))

Lisp> (SUBST 'ZERO NIL MTREE)      ; beware!!
((MAMMAL DOG CAT HORSE . ZERO)
 (DOG SPANIEL COLLIE TERRIER . ZERO)
 (CAT BURMESE . ZERO) . ZERO)

Lisp> (SUBST '(HORSE PINTO) '(CAT BURMESE)
         MTREE)
((MAMMAL DOG CAT HORSE)
 (DOG SPANIEL COLLIE TERRIER)
 (CAT BURMESE))
```

Note: In the last example, SUBST was not able to find the target list, (CAT BURMESE). This is because the test for equality used by SUBST is EQL and the list (CAT BURMESE) constructed with the quote mark in the input expression is not the same physical entity as part of the list called MTREE.

MEMBER requires two arguments: an item being tested for membership, and a list. If the item is found to be a top-level element of the list, MEMBER returns *the rest of the list,* beginning with the item. If the item is not found, MEMBER returns NIL. (Hence, despite its nonconformist name, MEMBER is a predicate.)

```
Lisp> (MEMBER 4 '(1 (2 3) 4 5) )
(4 5)
Lisp> (MEMBER 2 '(1 (2 3) 4 5) )
NIL                  ; not a top-level element
Lisp> (MEMBER 'A '(A B A C A D) )
(A B A C A D)        ; finds first occurrence
```

Note: The MEMBER function is also using the EQL predicate for its comparisons – this should always be borne in mind.

Arrays
The maximum rank and maximum size of arrays in Common Lisp are specific to the implementation. They may be examined by looking at the values assigned to the following system constants:

ARRAY–RANK–LIMIT   (max rank of array)
ARRAY–DIMENSION–LIMIT (max size of individual dimensions of any array)
ARRAY–TOTAL–SIZE–LIMIT (max number of elements in any array)

Array creation

When creating an array, we must give the intended dimensions. The function required is **MAKE—ARRAY,** for example:

    (MAKE—ARRAY '(4 2 3))
    creates a three dimensional array having 24
    elements.

N.B. To 'name' the array for future reference we
would need to use SETQ or other binding:
(SETQ A (MAKE—ARRAY '4 2 3)))

There are several options which can be specified when creating an array:

:INITIAL—ELEMENT   (keyword)
Enables initialisation of every element in the created array to be given the same value.

    Lisp> (MAKE—ARRAY '(2 3) : INITIAL—ELEMENT 0)
    #2A((0 0) (0 0))

:INITIAL–CONTENTS (keyword)

:INITIAL–CONTENTS and :INITIAL–ELEMENT are
mutually exclusive. This argument may be used to
initialise the contents of an array. The value should
be a nested structure of sequences. The number of
top-level elements must correspond to the first
dimension; each element must be a nested structure
for an array whose dimensions are the remaining
dimensions, and so on.

```
Lisp> (MAKE–ARRAY '(3 2)
   :INITIAL–CONTENTS   '((1 4) (4 9) (9 16)) )
#2A((1 4) (4 9) (9 16))
Lisp> (MAKE–ARRAY '(4 2 3) :INITIAL–CONTENTS
      '(((APPLE PEAR PEACH)
        (EGG HAM CRESS))          ; 2 × 3 array
       ((BOOK CLIP CUP)
        (PEN SLIDE STAPLE))       ; 2 × 3 array
       ((WATCH PAPER LAMP)
        (FIRE CLOCK BOOK))        ; 2 × 3 array
       ((TRAY BOX BANK)
        (PIN SABRE MIRROR)) ))    ; 2 × 3 array
#3A (...)
```

:ADJUSTABLE (keyword)

If the value specified here is non-NIL, then it will be
possible to alter the size of the array dynamically
after creation. Default is NIL.

:FILL—POINTER   (keyword)

This argument may only be supplied if the array is one-dimensional. The argument should be an integer between zero and the length of the array (both inclusive) and initialises the position of the fill-pointer. The fill-pointer is the number of 'active' or 'filled-in' elements, and makes it easy incrementally to fill in the contents of a one-dimensional array.

```
Lisp> (MAKE—ARRAY 6    ; parentheses
                        ; unnecessary for 1-d
       :INITIAL—CONTENTS '(JACK QUEEN ACE NIL
                                        NIL NIL)
       :FILL—POINTER 3)
     #(JACK QUEEN ACE)    ; only the active part
                          ; shows
```

Array access

AREF

This is the function used to access the elements of an array. It completely ignores any fill-pointer associated with the array. Its form is:

```
(AREF array sub1 sub2 ... subN)
```

The number of subscripts must equal the rank of the array. Each subscript must be a non-negative integer less than the corresponding array dimension.

N.B. The 'origin' of the array subscripting is at zero.

```
Lisp> (SETQ X (MAKE–ARRAY '(2 3)
  :INITIAL–CONTENTS '((A B C) (D E F)) ) )
#2A((A B C) (D E F))
Lisp> (AREF X 0 0)
A
Lisp> (AREF X 1 2)
F
Lisp> (AREF X 0 2)
C
Lisp> (AREF X 1 0)
D
```

It would be an error to request (AREF X 1 3) or (AREF X 2 1) or (AREF X 2 3) since these calls contain references to subscripts outside the bounds of the array.

The AREF access function is used in conjunction with SETF to update (destructively) the array elements.

```
Lisp>(SETF (AREF X 0 0) 'P)
P
Lisp> X
#2A((P B C) (D E F))
```

Array information

The following examples illustrate functions which produce interesting information concerning existing arrays:

```
Lisp> (SETQ M (MAKE–ARRAY '(8 3 5 6 9)) )
#5A (...)    ; a null 5-dimensional array
Lisp> (ARRAY–RANK M)
5
Lisp> (ARRAY–DIMENSION M 0)
8
Lisp> (ARRAY–DIMENSION M 1)
3
Lisp> (ARRAY–DIMENSION M 2)
5
Lisp> (ARRAY–DIMENSIONS M)
5
Lisp> (ARRAY–TOTAL–SIZE M)
6480
Lisp> (ARRAY–IN–BOUNDS–P M 7 2 4 5 8)
T
Lisp> (ARRAY–IN–BOUNDS–P M 7 2 5 5 8)
NIL    ; 3rd subscript out of bounds
Lisp> (ADJUSTABLE–ARRAY–P M)
NIL    ; did not specify :ADJUSTABLE non-NIL
```

Changing the dimensions of an arry

This is only permitted for an array A if (ADJUSTABLE–ARRAY–P A) returns T. The *rank* of an array cannot be changed: a 2-dimensional array cannot become 1-dimensional or 3-dimensional.

The function in question is **ADJUST–ARRAY**; its options are very similar to those of MAKE–ARRAY. Only interesting differences are noted here.

The dimensions specified to ADJUST–ARRAY are the required new dimensions; remember that the rank may not be changed.

```
(SETQ A (MAKE–ARRAY '(4 2 3) : ADJUSTABLE T))
(SETQ A1 (ADJUST–ARRAY A '(7 2 5)) )
```

This adjustment is a surgical operation: in creating array A1 we have asked for an adjustment of A. When this operation is carried out, A itself is changed. So after the above operations we will observe the following result:

```
Lisp> (ARRAY–DIMENSIONS A)
(7 2 5)
```

If the :INITIAL–ELEMENT option is provided to ADJUST–ARRAY, any elements not within the bounds of the original array are initialised.

If the :INITIAL–CONTENTS option is provided, the contents of the original array are completely overwritten.

If :FILL–POINTER is specified, the fill pointer is reset as directed. This is only permitted if the original array had its own fill-pointer.

Vectors

A vector is a one-dimensional array, and may therefore have a fill-pointer. Vectors can, of course, be manipulated using the array functions, but there is another set of functions which one may apply. A vector can be described as a *sequence* and functions applicable to sequences are described in the section entitled Sequence Operations below.

A particularly important subclass of vectors are the *strings*. These are specialised vectors whose elements are characters. String-specific functions are described in the section entitled String Operations on p. 96.

Sequence Operations

These operations are applicable either to lists or to vectors; both of these structures are sub-classes of *sequences*.

Simple functions

ELT requires two arguments; a sequence and an index. It returns the appropriate element.

```
Lisp> (SETQ EXLIST '(A C G T T A A))
(A C G T T A A)
Lisp> (SETQ EXVECT (MAKE-ARRAY 6
:INITIAL-CONTENTS '(2 3 5 7 11 13)) )
#(2 3 5 7 11 13)
Lisp> (ELT EXLIST 1)
C       ; indexed from zero
Lisp> (ELT EXVECT 5)
13
```

Note: ELT does not observe the fill-pointer in vectors which have a fill-pointer.

SETF may be used with ELT to replace destructively a sequence element. This will work irrespective of any fill-pointer position.

LENGTH returns the length of the sequence. If the sequence is a vector with a fill-pointer, the 'active length' is returned.

```
Lisp> (SETQ EXVECTF (MAKE-ARRAY 6
: INITIAL-CONTENTS '(2 3 5 0 0 0)
:FILL-POINTER 3) )
#(2 3 5)
Lisp> (LENGTH EXVECTF)
3
```

SUBSEQ returns a copy of a subsequence of the sequence given. The start position is always specified; specification of the end position is optional. The default end position is the length of the submitted sequence.

```
Lisp> (SUBSEQ EXLIST 3)
(T T A A)
Lisp> (SUBSEQ EXVECT 0 2)
#(2 3)
```

Note that the end position argument is not an index to the sequence. It refers to the *length* of the original sequence up to which the operation is to be performed.

REVERSE produces a new sequence of the same kind as that submitted, but the elements are in reverse order.

```
Lisp> (REVERSE EXLIST)
(A A T T G C A)
```

Modifying sequences

REMOVE <item> <sequence> returns a sequence from which all elements EQL to <item> have been removed.

```
Lisp> (REMOVE 'A EXLIST)
(C G T T)
```

REMOVE–DUPLICATES removes all duplicate
occurrences of the elements in the sequence.

```
Lisp> (REMOVE–DUPLICATES EXLIST)
(C G T A)      ; works from end of list
```

SUBSTITUTE is very similar to the SUBST operation
on lists. It replaces old sequence elements with new
ones.

```
Lisp> (SUBSTITUTE 91 5 EXVECT)
#(2 3 91 7 11 13)
```

N.B. None of these operations alter the value
bindings of their arguments.

Searching sequences

FIND searches for an item in a sequence; if
successful it returns the item: if not, it returns NIL.

```
Lisp> (FIND 'C EXLIST)
C
Lisp> (FIND 'D EXLIST)
NIL
```

Subsequence specifiers

All the functions given so far in this section can be modified to act upon sub-sequences of their arguments, by supplying them with extra parameters. This is done using the **:START** and **:END** keywords. The default for :START is 0, and the default for :END is the length of the original sequence. The returned value, however, includes those elements of the input sequence which were not affected by the operation.

```
Lisp> (REMOVE 'A EXLIST :END 3)
(C G T T A A)
Lisp> (REMOVE–DUPLICATES EXLIST :START 3)
(A C G T A)
Lisp> (FIND 2 EXVECT :START 3)
NIL
```

Concatenation

An arbitrary number of sequences can be concatenated into a sequence of a specified type, providing one does not ask the impossible! For example, strings can be concatenated into strings or vectors, but not into lists since strings are not a subtype of lists.

```
Lisp>(CONCATENATE 'STRING
    "EVERY CLOUD HAS" "A SILVER LINING")
"EVERY CLOUD HAS A SILVER LINING"
Lisp>(CONCATENATE 'STRING "NAME" "–"
    "OF" "–" "FUNCTION")
"NAME–OF–FUNCTION"
Lisp>(CONCATENATE 'LIST '(A B) '(C D) '(E F))
(A B C D E F)
```

Definition of New Functions

The definition of new functions is at the heart of
programming in Lisp.

To construct a definition, we need, minimally, to
inform the system of:

- the function name
- the sequence of arguments it will take
- instructions for manipulation of those arguments
- how the returned value is to be determined

The format for defining a new function is:

```
(DEFUN <name> (<arg1> <arg2> ... <argn>)
    <documentation string>
    <process instructions>
    <process instructions>...) )
```

The function DEFUN does not evaluate its arguments, and returns the name of the newly-defined function. The side effect of DEFUN is to attach a function binding to the symbol given as the function name, so when that symbol appears subsequently in the functional place in a list under evaluation, its arguments will be processed in accordance with the instructions specified in the function binding. The process instructions consist of zero or more s-expressions for evaluation.

Example
```
Lisp> (DEFUN LAST-EL (X)
"Returns the last top-level element of list"
   (CAR (REVERSE X)) )
LAST-EL

Lisp> (LAST-EL '(A B C) )
C
```

The documentation string should be used whenever possible to improve the clarity of Lisp programming. The string may include carriage returns; i.e. it may extend over several lines. It has no effect on the working of the function. It is an error to give more than one documentation string, but the existence of the string is optional.

When selecting a name for a function, the following points should be borne in mind.

- The chosen name should be reasonably meaningful and mnemonic; to create thirty or so functions called FN1, FN2, FN2, ... FN31 is unhelpful and extremely confusing if you are attempting to debug the program.

  A similar remark applies to the symbols used to represent the arguments in the function definition. If the first argument is to be an element and the second a nested list, then the choice of X1 and X2, or Y and Z, benefits no-one. Perhaps ITEM and NLIST or EL and LIST, would be better choices.

- There are certain **SPECIAL FORMS** known to the system: it is an error to attempt to redefine any of their names. These SPECIAL FORMS are listed below:

BLOCK	IF	PROGV
CATCH	LABELS	QUOTE
COMPILER-LET	LET	RETURN-FROM
DECLARE	LET*	SETQ
EVAL-WHEN	MACROLET	TAGBODY
FLET	MULTIPLE-VALUE-CALL	THE
FUNCTION	MULTIPLE-VALUE-PROG1	THROW
GO	PROGN	UNWIND-PROTECT

An existing function definition can be examined thus:

```
Lisp> (PPRINT–DEFINITION 'LAST–EL)
(DEFUN LAST–EL (X)
   "Returns the last top-level element of a list"
   (CAR (REVERSE X)))
```

The documentation string of the function may be retrieved thus:

```
Lisp> (DOCUMENTATION 'LAST–EL
        'FUNCTION)
   "Returns the last top-level element of a list"
```

This documentation string can be updated by using SETF with the DOCUMENTATION function.

Branching

In order to begin to write interesting functions in Lisp, we will need more tools than we already have. Possibly the most fundamental one is a function that enables branching to occur, giving us the facility to represent processes of the type

```
IF <test> THEN <action>
   ELSEIF  <test 1>  THEN <action 1>
   ELSEIF  <test 2>  THEN <action 2>

        .              .
        .              .
        .              .

   ELSE                <action N>
```

50

... which are familiar from other programming languages.

There are several functions available in Common Lisp which provide us with the ability to execute Lisp forms only when a certain condition obtains.

IF

This has the form
```
(IF <test> <then-action> <else-action>)
```

For example

```
(IF (ENDP MLIST) RESULT (+ 1 RESULT) )
```

When this is evaluated, the current binding of the variable **MLIST** is examined. If it is an empty list, then the entire IF-construct returns the value of the current binding of the RESULT variable. If MLIST is bound to a non-empty list, then the IF-construct returns RESULT + 1.

Note: Only *one* s-expression is allowed as the <then-action>. The <else-action> may be omitted entirely, but if present, it too must be a single s-expression.

```
(IF (ZEROP N) (* 2 (+ 1 N)) )
returns 2      if N = 0
       NIL    if N ≠ 0 (no <then-action>)
```

WHEN

The WHEN function has no <else-action>, but permits an arbitrary number of s-expressions to be evaluated when the <test> is non-nil.

   (WHEN <test> <then 1> <then 2> ... <then N>

e.g. (WHEN (ENDP MLIST)
        (PRINT "Function ends")
        (CLOSE INSTREAM)
        (REVERSE RLIST))

If MLIST is found to be the empty list, all the subsequent forms are evaluated. The value returned by the WHEN construct is the value of the *last* form evaluated, in this case the value of (REVERSE RLIST).

   Notice that this implies that, since the values produced by the preceding forms are lost, they (i.e. the PRINT and CLOSE forms) are included solely for their side effects.

   If MLIST is a non-empty list, no subsequent forms inside the WHEN construct are evaluated, and the whole construct returns NIL.

UNLESS

The UNLESS construct is the mirror-image of WHEN. It has the form

   (UNLESS <test> <else1> <else2> ... <elseN>)

If <test> returns NIL, then all subsequent forms ARE evaluated. (cf. WHEN; if a when-test returns NIL, nothing is evaluated.)

e.g. (UNLESS (EQUALP (READ) 'NO)
      (SETQ COUNT (+ 1 COUNT))
      (MUTATE DATATREE COUNT)
      (PRINT (TOP–OF DATATREE))
      DATATREE)

If the value of the function call (READ) is EQUALP to 'NO, no further evaluation of forms takes place, and the UNLESS construct returns NIL. For any other value of (READ) all subsequent forms are evaluated, and the value of DATATREE is returned by the UNLESS construct.

COND

This is the most general of the conditional functions; all the others are specialisations of COND, given a more pleasing syntax. A COND construct has the form:

    (COND (<test1> <action1A> <action1B> ...)
        (<test2> <action2A> <action2B> ...)
            .
            .
        (<testN> <actionNA> <actionNB> ...))

COND takes as many clauses as there are to be branches. Each clause is a list of one or more elements.

The first element is the condition (or test) of the clause. This is evaluated. If the value is NIL, control passes to the next clause. If the value is non-NIL, then the condition is judged to be successful, and the rest of the clause is evaluated. **No subsequent clauses will then be examined.** Although all the remaining elements in the successful clause are evaluated, it is only the last element whose value is returned by COND. Hence, any element lying between the first and the last elements in a clause can only be useful for its side effects.

If a clause has only one element, and its value is non-NIL, then that element also gives the returned value of the COND. So an expression can act both as a test and simultaneously represent its own result.

Example
```
Lisp> (DEFUN ADD—TITLE (NAME)
"This function returns a list of the submitted name,
with a title as the first element where appropriate.
e.g. Lancelot→ (Sir Lancelot)"
(COND ((MEMBER NAME KNIGHTS)
       (LIST 'SIR NAME))
      ((MEMBER NAME KINGS)
       (LIST 'KING NAME))
      ((MEMBER NAME QUEENS)
       (LIST 'QUEEN NAME))
      (T (LIST NAME)))) ; T as a test is always
                        ; successful

ADD—TITLE
```

```
Lisp> (SETQ KINGS '(ARTHUR))
(ARTHUR)

Lisp> (SETQ QUEENS '(GUINEVERE))
(GUINEVERE)

Lisp> (SETQ KNIGHTS '(GAWAINE LANCELOT
      GALAHAD))
(GAWAINE LANCELOT GALAHAD)

Lisp> (ADD–TITLE 'LANCELOT)
(SIR LANCELOT)              ; clause 1

Lisp> (ADD–TITLE 'MORDRED)
(MORDRED)                  ; clause 4

Lisp> (ADD–TITLE 'GUINEVERE)
(QUEEN GUINEVERE)          ; clause 3

Lisp> (ADD–TITLE 'ARTHUR)
(KING ARTHUR)              ; clause 2
```

Variable Binding and Scoping

There are two kinds of variable in Common Lisp; *special* (or dynamic) variables, and *lexical* (or *static*) variables. Both types have now been introduced, so we must now look more closely at the differences.

Until function definition was introduced, all the variables used were *special* variables. So assignments made at the top-level of the interpreter are assignments of values to special variables. The values assigned to such variables can be accessed and used by any Lisp form until either a new value is assigned to the variable, or the variable value is destroyed (usually by leaving the Lisp system). Special variables are said to have *dynamic* scope: they can be accessed from *any* piece of Lisp text as long as their binding is currently in effect.

In contrast, the value of a *lexical* variable can only be accessed from within a particular piece of text. The variables which act as arguments in function definitions fall into this category. For example:

```
Lisp>    (DEFUN DOUBLE (NUM)
         "Adds a number to itself"
         (+ NUM NUM) )
DOUBLE
```

NUM is a lexical variable; its value is bound only within the function body. When the function is called thus:

```
Lisp> (DOUBLE 6)
12
```

56

then NUM is bound to the value 6 while the process body of the function is evaluated, but after the DOUBLE function is exited, the variable is unbound. We cannot now reference that value:

```
Lisp> (CONS NUM '(1 2 3))
Error: Unbound variable NUM
```

However, the symbol NUM may also be assigned a global binding:

```
Lisp> (DEFVAR NUM 3)
3
```

NUM is now the name of a special variable whose value is 3.

```
Lisp> (+ 2 NUM)
5
```

If we now use the function DOUBLE:

```
Lisp> (DOUBLE 8)
16
```

... no confusion arises between the global value of 3 for the special variable, and the local binding of the value 8 to the lexical variable in the function definition. While the DOUBLE function is being executed, there are in fact two entities having the same name, NUM. The lexical variable NUM is said to *shadow* the special variable of the same name while function definition of DOUBLE is under evaluation.

It follows from this shadowing effect that we may not attempt to use the global binding of a variable in a function definition where it appears as a lexical variable.

e.g. a function to CONS the atom HEAD on to the front of any input list.

```
Lisp> (DEFVAR Y 'HEAD)
HEAD

Lisp> (DEFUN LISTCONS (Y
            (CONS Y Y))  ; we are trying to achieve
                         ; (CONS 'HEAD Y)
LISTCONS
```

Fairly obviously, the global binding of Y will never be used. The function would actually produce this kind of behaviour;

```
Lisp> (LISTCONS '(CHERRY COCONUT))
((CHERRY COCONUT) CHERRY COCONUT)
```

However, there are situations where the source of confusion is not so easy to spot. Functions are often called by other functions; it should always be remembered that the higher-level function affects the view of a variable perceived by the lower.

For example, consider two functions concerned with calculating simple interest and updating the balance with the interest calculated.

```
Lisp> (DEFUN INTEREST (BALANCE)
        (* BALANCE X) )            ; where X is the
                                   ; interest rate
INTEREST

Lisp> (DEFUN NEWBALANCE (X) ; X here
        (+ (INTEREST X) )          ; represents the
                                   ; old balance

NEWBALANCE
```

The NEWBALANCE function calls the INTEREST function: therefore INTEREST acts from a view of variable bindings which have already been modified by NEWBALANCE. The INTEREST function wants to use, presumably, the global binding of X; X is a *special variable* with respect to INTEREST. However, because INTEREST is called by NEWBALANCE, the value of X representing the rate will not be what we expect when the interest is calculated.

```
Lisp> (DEFVAR X 0.1)        ; interest rate of 10%
0.1

Lisp> (INTEREST 100)        ; no problem
10.0

Lisp> (NEWBALANCE 100) ; variable conflict!
10100.0
```

When NEWBALANCE is entered, X is lexically bound
to the argument provided; i.e. the value of X is 100 in
this environment. So when INTEREST is called, the
symbol BALANCE is lexically bound to the value of X,
100, which is correct; but the special variable X
representing the interest rate is bound in this
environment to 100 also.

So the effective calculation is

$$(+ 100 \text{ (INTEREST (100))} = (+ 100 (* 100 100))$$

which isn't at all what was meant.

To a large extent, this kind of variable conflict can
be avoided by sensible choice of variable names:
the following definitions not only read better, but
they also work properly.

```
Lisp> (DEFUN INTEREST (BALANCE)
         (* BALANCE INTEREST–RATE))
INTEREST

Lisp> (DEFUN NEWBALANCE (BALANCE)
         (+ BALANCE (INTEREST BALANCE) ))
NEWBALANCE
```

It is also worth remembering that while it would be obviously stupid to use X to represent different variables in two such closely related functions as INTEREST and NEWBALANCE, in a large program it may be extremely difficult to predict which functions can affect the environment for which others, because of the complexity of the interrelationships between functions.

Definition of extra local variables

It is often the case when programming that one would like the facility to define extra local variables, to store commonly used results of computations, or to act as accumulators, counters or record-keepers. There is a simple and elegant construct in Common Lisp which permits precisely this. Lexical variables may be defined, initialised and used, and when the construct is exited, the variables are restored to their former values, if any. This enables the programmer to use these extra variables in the secure knowledge that any global binding belonging to a special variable of the same name will neither affect the piece of Lisp text in question, nor be affected by it.

The construct we require for this enviable ability is called LET.

The syntax for LET is as follows:

```
(LET ((var1 value1) (var2 value2) ... (varN valueN))
  (process1)
  (process2)

        .
        .
        .

  (processM) )
```

When this construct is encountered, **value1** through **valueN** are evaluated (from left to right). Then the lexical variables **varJ** are bound to their corresponding values *in parallel*. The remaining forms inside the LET construct (here described by **processK**) are then evaluated in sequence. Upon leaving the LET construct, the variables **varJ** become unbound. The LET construct returns the value of the last form evaluated, i.e. **processM.**

Example of use
```
(DEFUN TEST (X)
(WHEN (EQUALP (CAR X) (CAR (REVERSE X)))
        (EQUALP (CADR X) (CADR (REVERSE
        X))) ) )
```

In order to avoid calculating (REVERSE X) twice, we could introduce another variable:

```
(DEFUN TEST (X)
  (SETQ Y (REVERSE X))
  (WHEN (EQUALP (CAR X) (CAR Y))
        (EQUALP (CADR X) (CADR Y))) )
```

However, Y is being used as a SPECIAL variable here; any value it may already have will be corrupted by the SETQ. So, it is infinitely preferable to employ a local variable:

```
(DEFUN TEST (X)
  (LET ((Y (REVERSE X)) )
  (WHEN (EQUALP (CAR X) (CAR Y))
        (EQUALP (CADR X) (CADR Y))) ))
```

It was noted above that LET binds values to the local variables in parallel; it is as though PSETQ were being used. If it is important that the local variables should be bound sequentially, then **LET*** should be employed. Except for the order in which the variables are bound, LET and LET* are identical. LET* binds its variables in the same manner as SETQ.

Recursion

It is often the case that in defining a function, we use
the function itself in the definition. This is most
commonly found when a function is taking apart
nested list structures. For example, the following
function is a predicate which returns T if its first
argument is present anywhere within its second,
list-type argument.

```
Lisp> (DEFUN PRESENTP (EL SET)
         (COND ((NULL SET) NIL)
               ((COND ((ATOM (CAR SET))
                       (EQL EL (CAR SET)))
                      ((PRESENTP EL (CAR SET)))))
               ((PRESENTP EL (CDR SET))) ))
```

PRESENTP has two points at which it can recurse. It
recurses using

   (PRESENTP EL (CAR SET))

because we don't know how deeply the lists are
nested; and it recurses using

   (PRESENTP EL (CDR SET))

because we cannot say in advance how long each
list or sublist will be.

When PRESENTP appears in the process body of
the definition, it is working on lists which are smaller

than the original list. Intuitively, we can see that this will make the recursion finite, and that it will eventually be stopped by Clause 1.

'Procedural Style' Control Structures

Blocks and exits

There may well be occasions when we wish to exit from the middle of a section of code without evaluating the remaining expressions. The constructs provided in Common Lisp to enable this are BLOCK and RETURN–FROM.

Each **BLOCK** is given a name (which is not evaluated). At any point within the code describing the BLOCK, evaluating the form

```
(RETURN–FROM <block-name>)
```

will cause an immediate transfer of control which exits from the named BLOCK. Other than this, the BLOCK simply consists of a series of s-expressions which are evaluated in the usual manner.

RETURN–FROM is allowed an optional second argument. If present, its value will be the value returned by the BLOCK construct if an exit is achieved by means of that particular RETURN–FROM.

The following example shows a BLOCK construct which has three possible exit routes; one natural and two premature.

```
(BLOCK EMPTY-SLOT-FILLER
  (LET ((SLOT (CAR (GET-SLOTS FRAME))))
            ;; local variable initialised
    (WHEN (VALUE-OF FRAME SLOT)
        (RETURN-FROM EMPTY-SLOT-FILLER
        'ALREADY-FILLED))
            ;; first premature exit, if a value already
            ;; present in the slot – 2nd arg is
            ;; returned by BLOCK
    (PUTSLOTVAL FRAME SLOT)
    (CREATE-VALUE FRAME SLOT))
            ;; value into empty slot
    (TIDY-UP FRAME SLOT)
            ;; housekeeping
    (WHEN (WARNING-FROM FRAME SLOT)
        (RETURN-FROM EMPTY-SLOT-FILLER
            'INAPPROPRIATE-VALUE))
            ;; second premature exit, if some
            ;; warning flag has been attached
            ;; to the slot
    (REMOVE (LIST FRAME SLOT) AGENDA)
            ;; a successful fill – do global
            ;; housekeeping
    (VALUE-OF FRAME SLOT)))
            ;; Natural block exit – value returned is
            ;; the value put into the slot.
```

When this construct is evaluated, it may return one of three possible values : ALREADY–FILLED ; INAPPROPRIATE–VALUE ; or the value placed into the empty slot.

The DEFUN form implicitly puts a BLOCK around the body of the function defined; this implicit BLOCK has the same name as the function. Therefore, one may use RETURN–FROM to exit prematurely from a function defined by DEFUN.

Iteration

It may well be that we wish to perform a process repeatedly, but that recursion is not a suitable technique. Common Lisp has several constructs available to facilitate various kinds of iteration.

Simple iteration
DOTIMES provides straightforward iteration over a sequence of integers. It has the form:

```
(DOTIMES ( variable  top-limit  result-expression )
         (process1)
         (process2) …
         (processN))
```

The loop variable is initialised to zero, and is incremented by 1 until (top-limit -1) is reached. For each value of the loop variable, all the included processes are evaluated. Finally, the result-expression is evaluated and returned as the value of the DOTIMES construct.

For example, here is a definition of the
FACTORIAL function using DOTIMES:

```
(DEFUN FACTORIAL (N)
    (LET ((RESULT 1))
        (DOTIMES (COUNT N RESULT)
        ;; for COUNT from 0 to N−1, giving
        ;; RESULT as ultimate value
    (SETQ RESULT (* RESULT (+ COUNT 1))) )))
        ;; multiplication factor runs from 1 to N
```

DOLIST is similar to DOTIMES, but instead of
providing a top-limit integer, we provide a list.
Initially, the loop variable is bound to the CAR of this
list, and subsequently bound to each element in turn.
All the included processes are evaluated for each
value of the loop variable. Finally, the result
expression is evaluated and returned as the value of
the DOLIST construct.

```
(DOLIST ( variable  list  result-expression  )
        (process1) ... (processN))
```

By way of example, we will use the ADD−TITLE
function and global variables defined in the section
entitled Branching on p. 54.

```
(DEFUN ADD−TITLE−TO−LIST (NAMELIST)
    (LET ((NEWLIST NIL))
        (DOLIST (NAME NAMELIST (REVERSE
                                NEWLIST))
            (SETQ NEWLIST (CONS (ADD−TITLE
                            NAME) NEWLIST)) )))
```

68

This yields:

```
Lisp> (ADD–TITLE–TO–LIST '(ARTHUR
        LANCELOT GUINEVERE))
((KING ARTHUR) (SIR LANCELOT) (QUEEN
GUINEVERE))
```

Had the result-expression been NEWLIST instead of (REVERSE NEWLIST), the following behaviour would have been obtained:

```
Lisp> (ADD–TITLE–TO–LIST '(ARTHUR
        LANCELOT GUINEVERE))
((QUEEN GUINEVERE) (SIR LANCELOT) (KING
ARTHUR))
```

General iteration
DO and **DO*** provide general iteration facilities with an arbitrary number of 'index variables'. DO and DO* are distinguishable only in the order in which their lexical variables are bound: this reflects the difference between LET and LET*.

The general form for the DO construct is

```
(DO ((var1 init1 step1)
     (var2 init2 step2) ....)
 (  end-test   result-expression   )
     (process 1) (process 2) …)
```

The first argument is a list of zero or more index-variable specifiers. Each specifier must contain the name of a variable, and the initial value it takes. The 'step' is an expression which is evaluted to give the new value of the variable in subsequent iterations. If a 'step' expression is not present, the variable is not updated by the DO structure when iteration occurs. However, the programmer is free to use a SETQ statement to change explicitly a variable value in the process body. For DO, the associated variables are bound (both initially and when stepping) in parallel, as if using PSETQ. For DO*, the variables are bound sequentially, as if using SETQ.

The second argument to the DO construct is a list whose first element is an end-test predicate. This is evaluated as soon as all the bindings are effected for a particular iteration. If the end-test returns NIL, then the process-body is entered; if non-NIL, then the result-expression is evaluated and the DO construct returns. This second argument can be thought of as an implicit COND structure; if the first element is non-NIL, *all* subsequent elements are evaluated and the value of the last is returned. However, unlike COND, if *no* result-expression is given, then the DO construct returns NIL. (COND would return the non-NIL value of the first element.)

For each iteration, the variables are appropriately bound, and the end-test evaluated. If the end-test predicate returns NIL, each of the process forms are evaluated. When this evaluation is complete, the cycle recommences. Several points concerning the DO process body should be noted:

- It is frequently empty; it is a common occurrence for all necessary computation to be described in the step expressions.
- An implicit BLOCK named NIL surrounds the entire DO form. Hence the function RETURN (=(RETURN–FROM NIL)) may be used to exit from the entire DO loop at any point. (This remark applies anywhere within the DO construct, although the use of RETURN in the index-variable specifiers or end-test clause would give an unpleasantly ill-structured function.)
- The process body of a DO construct constitutes an implicit **TAGBODY.** A TAGBODY construct is one in which any element which is NOT a CONS will be interpreted as a **tag** or marker. A tag is not evaluated; it serves as a location label for use with the function **GO.** When an expression

    (GO tag)

    is evaluated, control passes to the expression immediately following the named tag. Tags can be said to have lexical scope: a GO expression may not reference a tag outside the current TAGBODY environment.

E.g. DO construct process body:

```
... NEWTREE      ; tag
       (METAMORPHOSE MTREE)
       (WHEN (EQUALP (CAAR MTREE) 'STOP)
       (GO FINISH))
       (PRINT (BRANCH MTREE1))
       (GO NEWTREE)
   FINISH          ; tag
       (PRINT END–MESSAGE) ...
```

Clearly, spaghetti programming is easily achieved in Lisp using this kind of construct. Thus, it is recommended that a TAGBODY construct (implicit or otherwise) with its associated GO jumps should only be used if absolutely necessary; nine times out of ten, there is a better, clearer, more elegant, more efficient and altogether preferable method of achieving the desired effect.

The difference between DO and DO* can be seen by careful examination of the following two definitions of the factorial function. In both cases, notice that the process body is empty.

```
(DEFUN FACTORIAL (N)
   (DO ((COUNT N (–COUNT 1))
            ; loop variable
        (RESULT 1 (*RESULT COUNT)) )
            ; result accumulator
       ((= COUNT 1) RESULT) ))
            ; end-test and returned value
```

For the call (FACTORIAL 3) we have:

	COUNT	RESULT
1st iteration	3	1
2nd iteration	2	3
3rd iteration	1	6
returns RESULT i.e. 6		

N.B. Parallel binding of variables. In the expression
(* RESULT COUNT), the old value of COUNT is
referred to, not the new one.

```
(DEFUN FACTORIAL (N)
  (DO* ((COUNT N (− COUNT 1))
        (RESULT N (* RESULT COUNT)) )
    ((= COUNT 1) RESULT) ))
```

Now for the call (FACTORIAL 3) we have:

	COUNT	RESULT
1st iteration	3	3
2nd iteration	2	6
3rd iteration	1	6
returns RESULT i.e. 6		

Here the expression (*RESULT COUNT) refers to the
new value of COUNT, calculated by the expression
(− COUNT 1), since the bindings are effected
sequentially.

Indefinite interation

The **LOOP** construct is the simplest iteration facility. It controls no variables, and simply executes its body repeatedly. It has an implicit BLOCK named NIL around it, so it may be exited by using the RETURN function. It has the form:

```
(LOOP
   (process1) (process2) ... (processN))
```

If the LOOP returns at all, its value is given by the argument of the RETURN function wich enabled the exit to occur. For example:

```
(LOOP
   (PERMUTE LNEST)
   (WHEN (MEMBER TARGET (CAR LNEST))
         (RETURN (CAAR LNEST)) )
   (WIPE–OUT–HEAD LNEST) )
```

Property Lists

Symbolic atoms in Lisp may, as we have seen, have a value and a functional binding. We now introduce another Lisp expression which may also be bound to a symbol. This object is called the **property list.**

For example, on the property list of the symbol CAT we may find the following:

```
TYPE :    MAMMAL
COLOUR : (BLACK WHITE GINGER)
YOUNG :  KITTEN
GENUS :  FELIS
```

Each element of the property list consists of two parts: a symbol giving the name of the property, and an s-expression giving the value of that property. The term VALUE is used in a different sense here than when discussing value binding or assignment. For example, the value of the property TYPE on the property list of CAT is MAMMAL, but the global binding of the symbol TYPE is quite a separate entity, e.g. STENO, although both are referred to loosely as values.

The contents of a symbol's property list may be examined using the function SYMBOL-PLIST.

```
Lisp> (SYMBOL-PLIST 'CAT)
(TYPE MAMMAL COLOUR (BLACK WHITE
GINGER) YOUNG KITTEN GENUS FELIS)
```

In order to extract the value of a named property on a symbol's property list, we use the function GET.

```
Lisp> (GET 'CAT 'GENUS)
FELIS
Lisp>(GET 'CAT 'COLOUR)
(BLACK WHITE GINGER)
Lisp> (GET 'CAT 'FOOD)
NIL
```

Note that the last example demonstrates that there is no means of distinguishing the absence of a property on a property list from a property having the value NIL, using GET.

A property may be destructively removed from a property list using the function REMPROP.

```
Lisp> (REMPROP 'CAT 'GENUS)
T
Lisp> (SYMBOL-PLIST 'CAT)
(TYPE MAMMAL COLOUR (BLACK WHITE
GINGER) YOUNG KITTEN)
```

Note: REMPROP uses EQL to find the named property.

Given that we know that the access functions for property lists is GET, we can update or create the value of any property we choose, using SETF.

```
Lisp> (SETF (GET 'CAT 'COLOUR)
        'TORTOISESHELL)
TORTOISESHELL
Lisp> (GET 'CAT 'COLOUR)
TORTOISESHELL
Lisp> (SYMBOL-PLIST 'CAT)
(TYPE MAMMAL COLOUR TORTOISESHELL
YOUNG KITTEN)
Lisp> (SETF (GET 'CAT 'NAME) 'TIDDLES)
TIDDLES
Lisp> (SYMBOL-PLIST 'CAT)
(TYPE MAMMAL COLOUR TORTOISESHELL
YOUNG KITTEN NAME TIDDLES)
```

Clearly, a symbol which is the value of a property may have a property list of its own; it is easy to see, then, one way in which networks may be built up in Lisp.

Association Lists

While property lists are bound to an atom quite separately from that atom's value, association lists are structures which can be used as values – either values of properties, or as value bindings.

An association list, or a-list, is a list whose top-level elements are either lists or dotted pairs. The CAR of each of these CONSes is called the **key** and the CDR is called the **datum.** Given a **key,** the associated **datum** can be retrieved, and vice versa.

Retrieval of a datum is achieved by use of the **ASSOC** function.

Consider the following examples:

```
Lisp> (SETQ BATTLE13 '((HERO (ARTHUR))
                       (VILLAINS MORDRED
                        ACCOLON)
                       (LOCATION . CAMLANN)
                       ((PROBABLE DATE)
                       (683 . EV)) )
((HERO (ARTHUR) ...)
Lisp> (ASSOC 'LOCATION BATTLE13)
(LOCATION . CAMLANN)   ; Remember that
                       ; (CAR '(A . B))=A
                       ; (CDR '(A . B))=B

Lisp> (ASSOC '(PROBABLE DATE) BATTLE13)
NIL
```

A list cannot be used as a key here, because ASSOC is using EQL as the test to find the key.

```
Lisp> (ASSOC 'VILLAINS BATTLE13)
(VILLAINS MORDRED ACCOLON)

Lisp> (ASSOC 'HERO BATTLE13)
(HERO (ARTHUR))
```

Note that ASSOC returns the entire top-level element of the a-list; it does not strip off the key.

RASSOC is the reverse form of ASSOC; it should be provided with the datum and will return the key.

```
Lisp> (RASSOC 'CAMLANN BATTLE13)
(LOCATION . CAMLANN)
```

RASSOC also uses EQL to find a match so the *only* datum which can be found in our example is that belonging to LOCATION; i.e. the CDR is atomic, and hence matches when used with EQL. So, if one intends to use RASSOC for a-list ACCESS, one should be strict and employ only dotted pairs of symbols avoiding lists or dotted lists.

When the functions ASSOC and RASSOC are used, the answer returned is the first match encountered. Thus, if a key or datum appears more than once in the a-list, only the first value will be found. The others are SHADOWED by the first occurrence. This gives us the option of updating an a-list in a non-destructive manner, by adding new CONSes on to the front.

```
Lisp> (SETQ BATTLE 13 ( CONS
'(LOCATION . CADBURY) BATTLE13))
((LOCATION . CADBURY)
(HERO (ARTHUR))
(VILLAINS MORDRED ACCOLON)
(LOCATION . CAMLANN)
((PROBABLE DATE) (683 . EV)) )

Lisp> (ASSOC 'LOCATION BATTLE13)
(LOCATION . CADBURY)
```

The other answer is shadowed by this one.

There is a special function which achieves the CONS performed in the example above to update BATTLE13. It is called **ACONS**, and has the form

```
(ACONS key datum a-list)
```

So,

```
(ACONS 'LOCATION 'CADBURY BATTLE13)
= (CONS (CONS 'LOCATION 'CADBURY)
BATTLE13).
```

A SETQ must still be performed to update BATTLE13.

Association lists can easily be created from a list of keys and a list of data, using the function **PAIRLIS.**

```
Lisp> (PAIRLIS '(KEY1 KEY2 KEY3)
        '(D1 (D21 D22) (D31 D32)) )
((KEY1 . D1)
(KEY2 D21 D22)
(KEY3 D31 D32))
```

If an optional third argument is given to PAIRLIS, it must evaluate to an association list. The a-list created by PAIRLIS from the first two arguments will then be added on to the front of it.

N.B. PAIRLIS does not guarantee that the a-list constructed from its first and second arguments will have its elements in the same order as the list of the keys. So PAIRLIS cannot be used if elements for its use are intended to shadow other keys or data.

Iteration on List Elements

Mapping

It is not uncommon to wish to perform the same function on each element of a list in turn. There is a Lisp function which achieves precisely this. It is helpfully named **MAPCAR** since it maps a function on to the CAR of a list, then the CAR of the CDR, etc. MAPCAR returns a list, with one top-level element corresponding to each top-level element in the original list. The mapping between the source elements and the target elements is defined by the function name submitted as an argument to MAPCAR.

```
Lisp> (SETQ KNIGHTS '(GAWAINE LANCELOT
      GALAHAD BORS PERCEVAL TRISTRAM))
(GAWAINE LANCELOT GALAHAD BORS
PERCEVAL TRISTRAM)
Lisp> (DEFUN ADD–SIR (NAME))
      (LIST 'SIR NAME))
ADD–SIR

Lisp> (MAPCAP 'ADD–SIR KNIGHTS)
((SIR GAWAINE) (SIR LANCELOT) (SIR GALAHAD)
(SIR BORS) (SIR PERCEVAL) (SIR TRISTRAM))
```

MAPCAR will handle functions which take more than one argument. Ideally all the lists should be the same length; if not, the iteration terminates when the shortest list runs out, and excess elements in the other lists are ignored.

The use of MAPCAR with simple functions can aid
in filtering the elements of a list, for example:

```
Lisp> (SETQ FRENCH '(LANCELOT BORS))
(LANCELOT BORS)
Lisp> (DEFUN FIND-FRENCH (NAME)
        (IF (MEMBER NAME FRENCH)
            NAME
            NIL))
FIND-FRENCH

Lisp> (MAPCAR 'FIND-FRENCH 'KNIGHTS)
(NIL LANCELOT NIL BORS NIL NIL)
```

... which gets the message across but looks untidy.
We would like to get rid of the NIL's: it may be worth
remembering that

```
(APPEND NIL '(A) NIL '(B) NIL NIL '(C) NIL)
returns
(A B C)
```

There is a function which can exploit precisely this,
but first we must redefine FIND-FRENCH to obtain
an appropriate list structure:

```
Lisp> (DEFUN FIND-FRENCH (NAME)
        (IF (MEMBER NAME FRENCH)
            (LIST NAME) NIL))
FIND-FRENCH

Lisp> (MAPCAR 'FIND-FRENCH KNIGHTS)
(NIL (LANCELOT) NIL (BORS) NIL NIL)
```

The function **MAPCAN** is now applicable.

Lisp> (MAPCAN 'FIND–FRENCH KNIGHTS)
(LANCELOT BORS)

MAPCAN is a potentially dangerous function however, since it uses not APPEND, but another function called NCONC, which 'surgically' alters the lists which are submitted to it as arguments. NCONC and other surgical functions are described in the section entitled List Surgery on p. 84.

MAPCAR and MAPCAN both have complementary functions called, respectively, **MAPLIST** and **MAPCON.** They behave in a manner very similar to MAPCAR and MAPCAN, but apply the given function to successive CDRs of the argument lists, instead of successive CARs.

All four functions described so far in this section are used when the returned values accumulated during execution are of importance. However, it is not uncommon to wish to peform such iteration, yet to be uninterested in the values returned. In such a case, the CAR- and CDR-accessing mapping functions are, respectively, MAPC and MAPL. These can be used only when the importance of the submitted function lies in its side effects, not its returned values.

Applying a function to a list

Given a function name and a list of elements, we can call up the function to take the elements of the list as arguments. This is effected using **APPLY**.

The first argument of APPLY is a function name, and its second is a list. APPLY effectively makes the function name into the first element of the proffered list, then evaluates the whole thing.

```
Lisp> (APPLY '+ '(1 3 5 7))
16
```

Clearly, (+ '(1 3 5 7)) is not legal syntax, since + expects numbers, not lists, as arguments. So APPLY has provided us with a way of effecting (+ 1 3 5 7) when (+ '(1 3 5 7)) was submitted.

List Surgery

RPLACA surgically replaces the value of the CAR of a list, e.g.

```
Lisp> (RPLACA 'CAI KNIGHTS)
(CAI LANCELOT GALAHAD BORS PERCEVAL
TRISTRAM)

Lisp> KNIGHTS
(CAI LANCELOT GALAHAD BORS PERCEVAL
TRISTRAM)
```

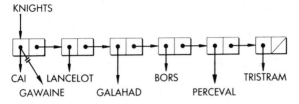

RPLACA is a mnemonic for replace CAR.

In an analogous fashion, **RPLACD** surgically replaces the value of the CDR of a list.

    Lisp> (SETQ KINGS '(ARTHUR))
    (ARTHUR)

    Lisp> (RPLACD KNIGHTS KINGS)
    (CAI ARTHUR)

    Lisp> KNIGHTS
    (CAI ARTHUR)

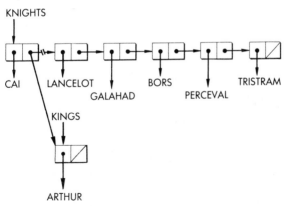

NCONC is a function which appears to behave very much like APPEND.

```
Lisp> (SETQ A '(APPLE APRICOT))
(APPLE APRICOT)
Lisp> (SETQ B '(BEAN BANANA))
(BEAN BANANA)
Lisp> (NCONC A B)
(APPLE APRICOT BEAN BANANA)
Lisp> B
(BEAN BANANA)
Lisp> A
(APPLE APRICOT BEAN BANANA)
```

The value binding of A has been altered. NCONC has altered the last list cell of A, so that it now contains a pointer to the first list cell of B.

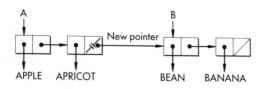

Anonymous Functions

When we use MAPCAR or similar functions which use a function name as one of their arguments, we may find it necessary to define and name a function which will only be used in that particular context; we may never need to reference it again. So, it seems to be something of a waste of time and storage to name it and file the functional definition away permanently.

It is in situations like this that we find anonymous function definitions useful.

We could define a function to be used with MAPCAR which puts SIR in front of each element of knights: such a function would be defined:

```
Lisp> (DEFUN ADD–SIR (NAME)
         (LIST 'SIR NAME))
ADD–SIR
```

We could then use ADD–SIR with MAPCAR. The alternative is to use the **LAMBDA** marker with the body of the function definition:

```
Lisp> (MAPCAR '(LAMBDA (NAME)
         (LIST 'SIR NAME)) KNIGHTS)
((SIR CAI) (SIR ARTHUR))
```

Note: **LAMBDA** is not a function. It is a symbol which has a special meaning within Lisp. Hence we must *quote* LAMBDA to prevent a search for its function binding. (There is in fact no reason – except clarity – why we should not choose the symbol LAMBDA to be the name of a user-defined function).

A Lambda-expression can, in fact, be used anywhere one might legitimately expect a function name. Note, however, that one cannot use this dodge when a recursive function is involved, because its very anonymity prevents the programmer from referring to the function in the process body.

Function Definitions Revisited

So far, when defining functions, we have been forced to declare the exact number of arguments which the function will accept. If we define:

(DEFUN EXFUN (A B C) ...)

then an error will result if we supply less than or more than three arguments. In this section we will consider how to

- define *optional* parameters, which may or may not be present when the function is called

- supply default values for these optional parameters, for use in cases where values are not provided when the function is called

- check during execution whether the value in use for an optional parameter is a default, or was supplied externally

- deal with any arguments which are neither *required,* nor defined to be *optional.*

Information about parameters other than the usual *required* ones is also carried in the parameter specifier list of a function definition. Two keywords may appear in the list, **&OPTIONAL** and **&REST**. So the general form of a function definition now looks like:

```
(DEFUN   name
     (var1 var2 ... varj ...
     &OPTIONAL opvarK (opvarL opinitL svarL) ...
     &REST restvar)
     ...)
```

The parameters **varj** are *required* parameters, and must all be specified to the left of the &OPTIONAL keyword. The parameter specifiers following the &OPTIONAL keyword describe the optional parameters of the function. They must all be specified to the left of the &REST keyword. The *single* parameter **restvar** follows the &REST keyword.

N.B. The keywords &OPTIONAL and &REST are not themselves parameters; when the function is called, nothing is bound to these symbols. They are simply flags which control the use of the parameter specifiers which follow them.

&OPTIONAL

A function may have any number (zero or more) of optional parameters. The general form of their specification is to describe each one by a structure:

    (opvar opinit svar)

opvar represents the name of the optional parameter. **opinit** is a Lisp expression which can be evaluated to produce an initial value for **opvar.** This is only actually done if the function is called without a value for this optional parameter; if a value is externally supplied, it will of course be bound to **opvar**. So **opinit** represents a means of supplying a default value to optional parameters. **svar** is called a *supplied–p* parameter, and holds information on whether or not the value bound to **opvar** originated from outside the function (i.e. externally supplied or default). **svar** is bound to NIL if **opinit** was evaluated (i.e. **opvar** has default value), or is bound to T if a value was supplied for **opvar.**

The **svar** specifier can be omitted if preferred, leaving the optional parameter specifier as (opvar opinit). If **opinit** is omitted, the parameter specifier may be written without the parentheses. In this case, if no value is externally supplied, **opvar** will be bound to NIL.

Example
```
(DEFUN EXFUN
   (V1 V2 &OPTIONAL (OP1 (LIST V1 V2) SUPP1
      OP2)
   LIST V1 V2 OP1 SUPP1 OP2) )

Lisp> (EXFUN 2 3)
(2 3 (2 3 ) NIL NIL)
Lisp> (EXFUN 2 3 4)
(2 3 4 T NIL)
Lisp> (EXFUN 2 3 '(2 3))
(2 3 (2 3) T NIL)
Lisp> (EXFUN 2 3 '(2 3) 'APPLE)
(2 3 (2 3) T APPLE)
```

&REST

Any arguments supplied to the function, which
remain after the required parameters have been
bound and the optional parameters have been
bound, are made into the elements of a list, and that
list is bound to the single **restvar** parameter which
follows the &REST keyword. If arguments are still
available and no &REST parameter is present, it is an
error. (The function has been called with too many
arguments.) The elements of the list bound to
restvar can be accessed using the usual CAR and
CDR operations. It is quite permissible (and quite

common) to find a function which uses the &REST
parameter, but does not have any parameters
controlled by the &OPTIONAL keyword.

Example
```
(DEFUN EXFUN
  (V1 V2 &OPTIONAL OP1 &REST OTHERS)
  (LIST V1 V2 OP1 OTHERS) )
Lisp> (EXFUN 1 2)
(1 2 NIL NIL)
Lisp> (EXFUN 1 2 3)
(1 2 3 NIL)
Lisp> (EXFUN 1 2 3 4 5 6 7 8)
(1 2 3 (4 5 6 7 8))
```

Macro Definition

A **macro,** like a function, is a named operation in
Common Lisp. In source code a macro call looks
much like a function call: for example SETF is
actually a macro, whereas SET is a function; the
programmer is not aware of any fundamental
difference when using them.

However, there *is* a fundamental difference
between functions and macros. When a function is
called, its variables are bound to the arguments
presented. The s-expressions which form the body of
the function definition are then evaluated in an
appropriate sequence, and the value of one of the
constituent s-expressions is returned by the function.

A macro behaves differently. Macros exploit the fact that in Lisp, data and procedures use the same basic representation, i.e. the list. So a macro assembles a tailored list, using the arguments supplied. This list forms the definition of an s-expression which can itself then be evaluated to give the final value of the macro call. The first evaluation is called the **macro expansion** phase.

The great benefit of the use of macros is only felt when a Lisp program is compiled and executed rather than interpreted. When compiling a program, a macro definition must always be presented *before* any reference to the macro in other definitions. (This restriction does not apply to functions.) This allows the compiler to perform the macro expansion, and then actually to insert the expansion code in place of the macro name in subsequent calls to the macro. This avoids the overhead of accessing a definition when its name is encountered, and greatly increases the efficiency of the program.

When we try to write a macro definition, there are two basic items which we need to be able to write down:

- an example of a call to the macro
- the code which we would like the macro to produce for our example.

For example, we wish to write the macro **PUSH** (although in fact this is provided by Common Lisp anyway!). PUSH will take two arguments, an item and a stack – in this case represented by a list; the head of the list being the top of the stack. So a call to PUSH could be

    (PUSH 'A STACK); where STACK evaluates to a
    list.

The code we wish to produce would be, say,

    (SETQ STACK (CONS 'A STACK))

Armed with this information, we can now attempt the macro definition.

Macros are defined using **DEFMACRO.** This is itself a macro, and has a syntax very like that of DEFUN.

Remember that we are trying to produce the expression

    (SETQ STACK (CONS 'A STACK)).

We then write:

    (DEFMACRO PUSH (ITEM STK)
      '(SETQ ,STK (CONS ,ITEM ,STK)))

The strange punctuation requires explanation. The backquote character ` acts like the quote character ', except that it allows us to nominate expressions *inside* the quoted form which *are* to be evaluated. The forms to be evaluated are then prefixed with a comma.

So if STACK has the value (B C D), the call (PUSH 'A STACK) has the following effect:

ITEM is bound to (QUOTE A)
STK is bound to STACK.

Then '(SETQ ,STK (CONS ,ITEM ,STK)) evaluates to

(SETQ STACK (CONS (QUOTE A) STACK))

is evaluated, giving

(A B C D)

as its value, and as a side effect altering the value of STACK.

Points to note:

- DEFMACRO is like DEFUN in that it may contain many s-expressions in its body. The *last* of these yields the form recognised as the macro expansion.

- Any expression which is legitimate for a DEFUN body is legitimate for DEFMACRO; we can use LET, BLOCK, DO etc., as we wish. Similarly we may use &OPTIONAL and &REST in the macro parameter list just as for DEFUN.

The function **MACROEXPAND** will take a *macro call* as an argument and return the approprite macro expansion.

```
Lisp> (MACROEXPAND (PUSH 'A STACK))
(SETQ STACK (CONS (QUOTE A) STACK))
```

String Operations

Strings are specialised vectors whose elements are characters. String operations generally operate only on the active portion of a string (below the fill pointer). Strings are written inside doubel quotes. The generic sequence functions described in pp. 42–47 can all be applied to strings.

String access

To access a single string character of a string, the function **CHAR** is used.

```
Lisp> (CHAR "This is a string" 0)
#\T
Lisp> (CHAR "This is a string' 5)
#\i
```

Note: the prefix #\ indicates a character literal.

SETF may be used with CHAR to replace (destructively) characters within the string.

String comparison

There are two groups of string comparison functions;
those which are case-sensitive, and those which are
case-insensitive. In both groups, subsequences can
be specified as was done for sequences (*see* p. 46).
There we used the keyword parameters :START and
:END. However, since we are comparing *two* strings,
we must use four keywords; :START1, :END1,
:START2 and :END2. The first pair refer to the first
argument, the second pair to the second argument.

Case-sensitive comparisons
```
Lisp> (STRING= "TOP" "TOP")
T
Lisp> (STRING= "TOP" "Top")
NIL
Lisp> (STRING= "together" "frog"
  :START1 1 :END1 3 :START2 2)
T
Lisp>+ (STRING> "STARTUP" "START")
5      ; true, returns length of common prefix
Lisp> (STRING> "START" "STARTUP")
NIL
```

The functions STRING<, STRING>=, STRING<=,
STRING/= (not equal to) conduct the appropriate
tests, and return a value in the same way as
STRING>, i.e. NIL if false, and length of common
prefix if true.

Case-insenstive comparisons
These functions are exactly analogous to the case-sensitive ones.

STRING–EQUAL	STRING–NOT–EQUAL
STRING–LESSP	STRING–NOT–LESSP
STRING–GREATERP	STRING–NOT–GREATERP

Input and Output Functions

Loading Lisp programs

When a file is loaded, each s-expression is read in and evaluated. The expressions which constitute a program will be DEFUN, DEFMACRO, DEFSTRUCT etc. forms. The Lisp loading function is **LOAD,** and its argument is a file name.

(LOAD "CAMELOT")   looks for a Lisp source
                          file called CAMELOT

Input

READ reads the next s-expression from the terminal. From the user's viewpoint, the system waits, giving no prompt. The value of the READ function, which takes no arguments, becomes equal to the input s-expression.
READ–LINE is used to get a line of input from the terminal. It returns the line as a character string, without the new-line character.

Output

PRIN1 and **PRINC** output the s-expression given as their argument, to the terminal. PRIN1 displays it in a form which is intended to be understandable to the READ function; PRINC produces a display for human consumption. Both functions return the s-expression given as the argument.

TERPRI requires no arguments, causes a 'new-line' on the terminal, and returns NIL.

PRINT is a composite function of TERPRI and PRIN1, followed by a printed space, i.e.

$$(PRINT X) = (TERPRI) (PRIN1 X) (PRINC " ")$$

WRITE—LINE is the inverse of READ—LINE; its argument is a string which is displayed on the screen without the double quotes, and is followed by a new line.

Data Structure Definition and Access

A facility is available in Common Lisp for the user to create a new 'data types'; complex structures which can be very simply defined and accessed.

It is possible, for example, to define a structure called a BOOK; let us say that this will always contain four elements:

- the title
- the publisher
- the author
- the publication date

If we represent these elements in a list, we could write suitable access functions:

```
Lisp> (SETQ BOOK1 '("HEAT" "M NELKON"
   "BLACKIE" 1971))
(...)
Lisp> (DEFUN BOOK–TITLE (BOOK)
     (CAR BOOK))
Lisp> (DEFUN BOOK–AUTHOR (BOOK)
     (CADR BOOK))
BOOK–AUTHOR
Lisp> (BOOK–TITLE BOOK1)
"HEAT"
```

Structure definitions enable us to short-circuit this process; they also remove the problem of making sure that all books have the sequence elements describing them in the correct order.

We can use the DEFSTRUCT operation to define BOOK:

```
Lisp> (DEFSTRUCT BOOK
   "This structure describes all published books"
     TITLE AUTHOR PUBLISHER
     PUBLICATION–DATE)
BOOK
```

Once this definition has been evaluated, we have many useful functions at our disposal.

Creation of BOOK-type objects

A constructor function called **MAKE–BOOK** is defined by the system. The attribute or 'slot' names are used as keyword arguments, thus

```
Lisp> (SETQ BOOK1
        (MAKE–BOOK  :TITLE "HEAT"
                    :AUTHOR "M NELKON"
                    :PUBLISHER "BLACKIE"
                    :PUBLICATION–DATE
                    1971) )
#S(BOOK :TITLE "HEAT" :AUTHOR "M NELKON"
        :PUBLISHER "BLACKIE"
        :PUBLICATION–DATE 1971)
```

N.B. It is not obligatory to fill all the possible slots when constructing the instances of the structure. The prefix #S denotes an instance of a structure.

Access functions to BOOK-type objects

The slot names are prefixed by the structure name and a hyphen, to produce access function names:

```
Lisp> (BOOK–PUBLISHER BOOK1)
"BLACKIE"
```

All the access functions thus created take one argument which must evaluate to an object of type BOOK.

Data type test

A predicate **BOOK—P** is created.

```
Lisp> (SETQ TOME '("EXODUS" "MOSES"
      "GOD" —1500))
TOME
Lisp> (BOOK—P TOME)
NIL
Lisp> (BOOK—P BOOK1)
T
```

Modify slot values

SETF can be used in conjunction with the access
functions to change slot values.

We can take DEFSTRUCT a step further and use it to
define default values for slots. Here is an expanded
definition of BOOK:

```
(DEFSTRUCT BOOK "Describes all published
books"
  TITLE AUTHOR PUBLISHER
  PUBLICATION—DATE
  (BINDING 'PAPERBACK) )
```

The last slot definition is a list containing the slotname **BINDING**, and a Lisp expression which can be evaluated to give the default value for the slot. This default is only evaluated when MAKE–BOOK is called, *and* no value is presented to MAKE–BOOK for the BINDING slot.

```
Lisp> (SETQ BOOK2 (MAKE–BOOK
     :TITLE "LISP" :AUTHOR "D S TOURETZKY"
     :PUBLISHER "HARPER & ROW"
     :PUBLICATION–DATE 1984)
(...)
Lisp>( BOOK–BINDING BOOK2)
PAPERBACK
Lisp> (SETQ BOOK3 (MAKE–BOOK
     :TITLE "WHEN THE WIND BLOWS"
     :AUTHOR "R BRIGGS"
     :PUBLISHER "HAMISH HAMILTON"
     :PUBLICATION–DATE 1982
     :BINDING 'HARDBACK) )
(...)
Lisp> (BOOK–BINDING BOOK3)
HARDBACK
```

Dialects of Lisp

Lisp is a language which suffers from the lack of a universally recognised standard definition. Modern Lisp dialects are descended from Lisp 1.5, implemented in 1962 at Massachusetts Institute of Technology. Very many dialects are now in use, depending largely on which hardware is available.

The differences between various dialects are themselves irregular. For example, MacLisp, Franz Lisp and Lisp Machine Lisp all define functions using **defun,** just as described for Common Lisp in this handbook. However MacLisp integers are given in octal, Franz Lisp works entirely in lower case, and all except Common Lisp offer a type of function called a **fexpr,** which is not covered here. Another major dialect, Interlisp, uses a function called **defineq** instead of **defun.** Such examples are only a tiny fragment of the detailed differences between dialects.

Other dialects which may be encountered are UCI Lisp, TLC-Lisp, P-Lisp, Standard Lisp, Portable Standard Lisp, xlisp, ZetaLisp and SpiceLisp. Into this Tower of Babel has at last come a ray of hope in the guise of Common Lisp. Common Lisp is directly descended from MacLisp, one of the most important dialects. The definition of the language was published in 1984, and since then there seems to have been real movement towards employing this dialect as the de facto standard. Many sites have changed from other dialects to Common Lisp and its availability on IBM PCs, DEC machines (as Golden Common Lisp and VAXLisp respectively) and many others, bodes well for its future general acceptance.

Index

105